LESS STRESS MORE

Yes

Copyright © 2024 Nicholas Boothman
The scanning, uploading, and distribution of this book without permission is a theft of the author's intellectual property. If you would like permission to use material from the book (other than for review purposes), please contact info@nicholasboothman.com
Thank you for your support of the author's rights.

ISBN 978-0-9958581-5-2
First printing April 20

When one door closes, another door opens, but often we look so long and so regretfully at the door that closed that we don't see the one that opened.

Alexander Graham Bell
INVENTOR OF THE TELEPHONE

Boothman is Dale Carnegie for a rushed era.
The New York Times

Training the New York SuperCops includes daily discussions on the works of Aristotle, H. G. Wells, and Nicholas Boothman.
The New Yorker

Contents

Part 1: The Stress Takedown 9

Chapter 1: The Red Alert   11

Chapter 2: Money!!!   19

Chapter 3: Trigger Point Zero   23

Chapter 4: The 60-Second Stress Buster   31

Chapter 5: Time Bandit Exposed   37

Chapter 6: The Power of "No"   45

Part 2: Reclaiming Your Yes..............................51

Chapter 7: The "Yes" Inventory   53

Chapter 8: Micro-Adventures   59

Chapter 9: The Done List Revolution   65

Chapter 10: Energy Vampires? Stake Them!   71

Chapter 11: The Art of Delegation   77

Part 3: Building a Stress-Resistant Life 83

Chapter 12: Sleep is Your Superpower — 85

Chapter 13: Fuel Your Fire — 91

Chapter 14: Movement as Medicine — 97

Chapter 15: The Mind Game Advantage — 103

Chapter 16: Digital Detox — 109

Part 4: The More Yes Multiplier.....................115

Chapter 17: Embrace The Unexpected — 117

Chapter 18: The Power of Connection — 123

Chapter 19: Small Steps, Big Wins — 129

Chapter 20: A Stress-Free Sanctuary — 135

Chapter 21: Cultivating Calm — 139

Chapter 22: Free Your Spirit — 143

LESS STRESS: MORE YES

Your brain plays tricks. Your body pays the price.

LESS STRESS: MORE YES

Part 1: The Stress Takedown

We all have a breaking point. A moment when life feels like way too much to handle. For Billie, a young woman whose story will resonate with many, that moment came when she realized she was constantly stressed and overwhelmed. But though this is Billie's story, its lessons are universal. This book is for anyone, regardless of age or gender, who has ever felt the crushing weight of modern life and yearned for a way to find more peace, joy, and fulfillment.

LESS STRESS: MORE YES

Chapter 1:
The Red Alert

The buzzing started low, a persistent hum beneath the surface. Like a mosquito you couldn't quite swat. Billie ignored it. She always did. Ignoring things was her superpower. Or so she told herself.

6:03 AM. The digital numbers on her alarm clock glowed a vengeful red. Another day. Another climb. Another mountain of... stuff. Stuff that needed doing. Stuff that screamed for attention. Stuff that felt like it was slowly crushing her.

She slapped the snooze button. Not once. Not twice. Three times. Each press a tiny act of rebellion against the inevitable. Five more minutes. Five stolen moments of oblivion before the onslaught began.

The hum intensified. It wasn't the clock. It was her. Her internal engine revving way too high, idling on fumes of anxiety and caffeine.

She finally dragged herself out of bed. The floorboards creaked a mournful protest. Just like her joints. Twenty-nine years old. Felt like sixty some mornings. The mirror confirmed the suspicion. Dark circles under her eyes. A faint line etched between her eyebrows – the permanent furrow of worry.

She splashed cold water on her face. The shock was momentary. The weariness lingered.

Downstairs, the coffee machine gurgled its morning song. A small comfort in the chaos. She poured a mug, black as night, strong enough to kickstart a dead battery.

Her phone buzzed on the counter. Email. Work. Already. Before the sun was even fully up.

Subject: URGENT – Project Phoenix Update Required ASAP.

ASAP. The four most terrifying letters in the English language. Her stomach clenched. Project Phoenix. The name sounded grand, like some mythical rebirth. In reality, it was a logistical nightmare, a tangled web of deadlines and demanding clients.

She skimmed the email. More problems. More fires to put out. More pressure.

The buzzing in her head was now a full-blown alarm. A red alert.

This was her life now, a constant state of low-grade panic, occasionally punctuated by spikes of full-blown dread. At twenty-eight, Billie had once envisioned a vibrant career, a life filled with creative pursuits and genuine connection. Instead, she found herself an Associate Marketing Manager at Veridian Solutions, a rising star in the tech landscape, or so the glossy company brochures proclaimed. Her initial enthusiasm had long since been eroded by the sheer, unyielding volume of work, the impenetrable corporate jargon, and a creeping sense that something was fundamentally off.

She thought back to last night. Dinner with friends. Supposed to be relaxing. Instead, her mind had raced a mile a minute, ticking off to-do lists, replaying conversations, anticipating tomorrow's disasters. She'd smiled and nodded, but she hadn't truly been present.

The laughter of her friends had sounded distant, muffled by the internal static.

Later, in bed, sleep had been a battlefield. Her thoughts had swirled, a relentless storm of worries. Did she lock the front door? Had she paid that bill? What if she messed up the presentation tomorrow?

She'd finally drifted off, only to be jolted awake by the same gnawing anxiety at 3 AM. Staring at the ceiling, the darkness amplifying her fears.

She looked around her apartment. Cluttered. Not hoarder-level, but definitely... chaotic. Piles of laundry waiting to be folded. Stacks of papers threatening to topple over. A visual representation of the mental clutter that filled her brain.

The buzzing intensified again. This time, it wasn't just in her head. Her phone was ringing. Her boss.

She took a deep breath. The coffee hadn't even hit her system yet, and she already felt drained.

"Morning, Julian," she said, trying to inject some semblance of energy into her voice.

Julian's voice on the other end was sharp, impatient. "Billie, about the Phoenix update..."

And just like that, the day began. The pressure cooker was on.

The commute was another layer of daily torment. The subway, a sardine can on wheels, amplified her already heightened senses. The clamor of conversations, the pungent mix of body odor and stale coffee, the jostling of bodies – it all contributed to the dull throb behind her eyes. She longed for the days when she could lose herself in a good book or simply watch the world go by, but those moments felt like a luxury from a past life.

Billie's cube, was a small island in a sea of identical workstations. Sticky notes littered her monitor. Her inbox a battlefield. Her calendar a dense block of back-to-back meetings.

"Billie, a moment?" Julian's voice, smooth as polished granite, cut through the office buzz. He stood by her cube, impeccably dressed, a faint smile playing on his lips.

"Of course, Julian," she said, her stomach clenching.

"Just checking in on the Phoenix report. We need it finalized by noon. The board presentation is moving up."

She blinked. "Noon? But I was expecting to have the full day, like we discussed yesterday."

Julian's smile didn't falter. "Agile, Billie, agile. We adapt. I have full faith in you. You're one of our strongest assets." He patted her shoulder. It felt like a like a claim of ownership. "I'll be in my office if you need anything."

He walked away, leaving her with a rising sense of panic. Noon. Six hours to finalize a report that required at least a full day. This wasn't just stressful; it felt deliberately punitive.

Around ten-thirty, she walked to the break-room. She refilled her water, trying to focus on the simple act, but her thoughts kept returning to the Phoenix report, the impossible deadline, Julian's unnerving smile. As she turned to leave, she overheard a snippet of conversation from two senior managers by the vending machine. "—metrics are through the roof. The stress levels are exactly where we need them to be for the next phase."

Back at her desk, the words echoed in her mind. "The stress levels are exactly where we need them to be."

Was it just corporate speak, a cynical reference to employee productivity under pressure? Or was there something more sinister at play?

This wasn't how it was supposed to be. She remembered a time, not so long ago, when she felt... lighter. More open. More willing to say "yes" to life's possibilities. Now, every invitation, every new request, felt like another weight added to the already crushing load.

She found herself saying "no" more and more. Not because she didn't want to, but because she simply didn't have the bandwidth. No to dinner with friends. No to that interesting new project. No to anything that required even a sliver of extra energy.

Her world was shrinking. Her horizons narrowing. All because of this relentless, suffocating stress.

She looked at her reflection again. The woman staring back was tired. Defeated. And a little bit scared.

This couldn't continue. Something had to change.

This wasn't about finding some mythical work-life balance. That felt like chasing a unicorn in a hurricane. This was about survival. About reclaiming her life, one small step at a time.

The red alert was blaring. And for the first time in a long time, She wasn't going to ignore it. She was going to fight back.

The first step? Recognizing the enemy. Understanding its tactics. Knowing what she was up against.

Stress. It wasn't just a feeling. It was a thief. Stealing her time, her energy, her joy. It was a saboteur, whispering doubts and fears, holding her back from the life she deserved.

And it was time to stop letting it win.

Right here. Right now.

The buzzing in her head finally started to subside, replaced by a flicker of something else. A spark of defiance. A tiny seed of hope.

This was the red alert. And Billie was finally ready to answer the call.

The fight for "Less Stress" and a resounding "More Yes" was about to begin. And she was in it to win.

Chapter 2: Money!!!

The rent was due. Again. The collection notice on the fridge wasn't just paper; it was a physical weight pressing down on her chest. Sleep was a luxury she could barely afford, both in time and in peace of mind.

Her mother's voice echoed in Billie's memory. Another doctor's appointment. Another bill Billie couldn't quite meet. The guilt was a constant gnawing ache, a fresh wave of anxiety washing over her.

Money? The silent killer, the invisible weight.

It burrows deep, poisoning your work, your home, even your health. And the research? It's stark. Women carry a heavier burden, their stress levels often outstripping men's. And financial worries? They're usually at the top of that poisonous list. The bills stacked on the counter, mocking your empty wallet. The kids needing things you can't afford. The weight of responsibility crushing your shoulders. You feel trapped.

So, did you pick up this book expecting miracles? Quick fixes? A secret handshake that makes your money problems vanish? Forget it. Less Stress: More "Yes" isn't that book. This isn't about making you rich. Not directly, anyway. No stock tips, no budgeting hacks, no magic formulas for landing that corner office.

This is bigger than your bank account. This is about your head. Your gut. It's about finding a way to soar above the suffocating grip of financial stress. You've got to deal with it, and the one way you absolutely cannot deal with it is with panic. Panic is the enemy of clarity, the thief of solutions. It shackles your mind, clouds your judgment, and keeps you stuck in a cycle of worry and inaction.

But, you're not powerless. In the pages that follow, you'll discover practical, actionable tools designed to help you regain control. Tools like the 60-Second Stress Buster, which isn't some esoteric meditation technique, but a simple, immediate way to take the edge off stress, to dial down the panic, and to create the mental space you need to solve things for yourself. This book is your guide to building resilience, one practical step at a time, so you can move from a state of overwhelm to one of empowered action.

Billie's story starts now. And maybe, just maybe, it's the beginning of yours too.

To help you gain awareness of your daily stress levels and identify patterns, here's a simple stress tracker.

Take a moment each day to jot down your score and any contributing factors. At the end of each day, or whenever you feel a moment of calm reflection, give your day a stress score from 1 to 5:

1: Zen Master. Today was incredibly calm and easy. I felt in control and positive.

2: Mostly Mellow. Some minor bumps, but overall, a good day with manageable stress.

3: A Bit Bumpy. I definitely felt some stress today. Things felt a little overwhelming at times.

4: High Alert. Today was quite stressful. I felt overwhelmed, anxious, or irritable for much of the day.

5: Full-Blown Frazzled. I felt completely overwhelmed and unable to cope. This was a very stressful day.

By regularly tracking your stress, you'll start to see patterns. Are certain days more stressful than others? Do specific situations or people consistently trigger higher stress levels? More importantly, you'll begin to identify what helps you shift from "less stress" to "more yes."

Start when you are ready.

Chapter 3: Trigger Point Zero

The meeting room was a pressure cooker. Polished mahogany table. Glaring fluorescent lights. And around it, the faces. Grim. Determined. Hungry.

Billie sat at the edge, notepad in hand, heart hammering a frantic rhythm against her ribs. Project Phoenix. Again.

Julian, a human caffeine IV drip, was pacing. "We're bleeding money," he barked. "Deadlines are slipping. Clients are circling like sharks. We need solutions. Now."

Solutions. The word hung in the air, heavy with expectation. Billie felt a familiar wave of nausea wash over her. This. This was one of her Trigger Points.

These high-stakes meetings. The constant pressure to perform. The fear of failure hanging over her like a guillotine.

She wasn't alone. Around the table, she saw the telltale signs. John, the usually unflappable accountant, was tapping his pen, a nervous tic. Maria, the marketing director, had a death grip on her coffee cup, knuckles white. Even Mark, the Energizer Bunny of stress, had a sheen of sweat on his forehead.

This wasn't just about Project Phoenix. It was about the entire company. The entire industry. The whole damn world, it seemed. Everyone was on edge. Everyone was running on fumes.

But Billie knew, deep down, that while the external pressures were real, the internal triggers were the most dangerous. The things that set off the chain reaction within her. The things that turned a manageable challenge into a full-blown panic attack.

She scribbled furiously in her notepad, not notes from the meeting, but her own personal inventory of stress bombs.

- Trigger Point #1: The Unrealistic Deadline. Julian's "ASAP" was a recurring nightmare. The constant pressure to deliver miracles on a shoestring timeline. It wasn't just about the work; it was about the feeling of being set up to fail.

- Trigger Point #2: The Perfection Trap. Her own relentless inner critic. The voice that whispered, "Not good enough," no matter how hard she worked. The fear of making a mistake, of falling short of some impossible standard.
- Trigger Point #3: The Toxic Relationship. Her sister, Brenda. A black hole of negativity and drama. Every phone call, every family gathering, left Billie feeling drained and depleted. Like she'd just run a marathon in quicksand.
- Trigger Point #4: The Information Overload. The endless barrage of emails, notifications, news alerts. The feeling of being constantly bombarded, of never being able to truly disconnect.
- Trigger Point #5: The Guilt Trip. The nagging feeling that she should be doing more. Working harder. Being more productive. The societal pressure to be a Superwoman,

juggling a million things without breaking a sweat.

She stared at the list. It was a rogues' gallery of stress triggers. Each one a potential landmine in the minefield of her life.

Julian was still talking, his voice rising. "We need to find a way to cut costs. Streamline processes. And we need it yesterday!"

Billie felt her pulse quicken. Her palms were sweating. The room seemed to be closing in on her.

This was it. Trigger Point Zero. The perfect storm. The convergence of all her stress bombs into one explosive situation.

She knew, in that moment, that she couldn't keep going like this. She couldn't keep reacting to these triggers like a puppet on a string. She had to take control.

But how?

The answer, she realized, wasn't to eliminate the triggers entirely. That was impossible. Life was full of deadlines, demanding bosses, and unavoidable challenges.

The key was to neutralize their power. To disarm them. To learn how to navigate these situations without losing her sanity.

She thought back to her grandfather, a grizzled old fisherman who had weathered countless storms at sea. He used to say, "The sea will always be the sea. But you can learn to sail."

That was it. She couldn't change the world. But she could change how she reacted to it.

She took a deep breath, the first one she'd taken all morning, it seemed. She felt of the air filling her lungs, expanding her chest, and then followed it down, willing her tummy to soften and rise with the gentle pressure. A slow, steady exhale followed, carrying with it the tension that had been clinging to her shoulders like a persistent shadow. Another inhale, long and deliberate, anchoring her in the present moment, an island of calm amidst the swirling thoughts.

It was a small act of defiance. A tiny assertion of control in the midst of chaos.

She looked around the room again. The faces of her colleagues. The pressure in the air.

They were all in the same boat. Struggling. Stressed. Trying to stay afloat in a sea of uncertainty.

But she didn't have to drown.

She made a decision. Right there, in that pressure-cooker meeting room. She was going to learn to sail.

She was going to identify her triggers. Understand their power. And find ways to defuse them.

It wouldn't be easy. It would take work. It would take practice.

But it was essential.

Her sanity, her health, her happiness depended on it.

The meeting droned on. Julian continued his tirade. But something had shifted within Billie.

She was no longer just a victim of her circumstances. She was a warrior. A strategist. A survivor.

She was taking back her life, one trigger point at a time.

And the first step was simply knowing her enemy. Knowing the specific things that set her off. Knowing the patterns of her stress.

It was a small victory, but it was a victory nonetheless.

She left the meeting feeling... different. Not exactly calm. Not exactly relaxed. But... empowered.

She had faced her Trigger Point Zero. And she had survived.

More than that, she had learned something. She had learned that stress wasn't some abstract monster. It was a collection of specific, identifiable triggers.

And once you knew your triggers, you could start to disarm them.

The fight was far from over. But Billie knew, with a newfound certainty, that she was on the right track.

She was learning to sail. And she was determined to navigate the storms ahead.

LESS STRESS: MORE YES

Chapter 4: the 60-Second Stress Buster

The elevator doors slid open. A wall of noise hit Billie like a physical blow. The din of the city. Honking taxis. Shouting vendors. The relentless, pulsing rhythm of urban chaos.

She stepped out, took a deep breath, and immediately regretted it. The air was thick with exhaust fumes and the smell of... something vaguely unpleasant.

Another day. Another gauntlet.

She was already on edge. The meeting with Julian had left her rattled. The image of her Trigger Point list was burned into her mind. She knew her enemy. Now, she needed weapons.

She needed something to fight back with. Something fast. Something effective.

She needed the 60-Second Stress Buster.

The concept was simple, almost deceptively so. When stress hit - and it would hit, no matter how hard she tried to avoid it - she needed a tool, a technique, a way to defuse the situation immediately.

Not hours later, after the damage was done. Not tomorrow, when she was already burned out. Right now. In the moment.

She walked briskly down the sidewalk, dodging the throngs of people. Her phone buzzed. Another email. Another demand.

Her shoulders tightened. Her jaw clenched. The familiar pressure building in her chest.

Time for the 60-Second Stress Buster.

She stopped. Right there on the crowded sidewalk. People swirled around her, oblivious to the internal battle she was waging.

She closed her eyes.

- Deep Breath #1: She inhaled slowly, deeply, filling her lungs and tummy with air. Not the polluted city air, but an imagined breath of fresh, clean oxygen. She held it for a count of four. Then exhaled slowly, deliberately, releasing the tension with her breath. She imagined the stress flowing out of her body, like dark smoke dissipating into the air.
- Repeat twice. With each breath, she felt a tiny sliver of the pressure release.

Sixty seconds. That's all it took. Three deep breaths.

It wasn't a miracle cure. The stress didn't vanish completely. But the edge was gone. The immediate panic had subsided. She felt... more grounded. More centered.

She opened her eyes. The city was still chaotic. The noise was still deafening. But she was different. She was... calmer.

She continued walking, her pace more measured now. She had a weapon. A simple, but powerful tool to fight back against the onslaught of stress.

She started to experiment.

Later that day, in another pressure-cooker meeting (this time with a client who seemed to enjoy making unreasonable demands), she felt the familiar tightness in her throat.

She excused herself. "Just need to grab some water," she said, her voice surprisingly steady.

In the hallway, she found a quiet corner. And she used the 60-Second Stress Buster.

Three deep breaths.

It worked again.

She returned to the meeting, her demeanor transformed. She was still assertive but she wasn't reactive. She wasn't on edge. She was in control.

The client, perhaps sensing the shift, seemed less... aggressive. The meeting ended without a full-blown meltdown.

Billie realized something profound. The 60-Second Stress Buster wasn't just about breathing. It was about creating a pause. An interruption in the cycle of stress.

It was about taking a moment to step back, to regain perspective, to choose how she wanted to respond, rather than simply reacting.

She started to incorporate other techniques into her 60-second arsenal.

- The Mental Reset: She would visualize a peaceful scene. A quiet beach. A snow-capped mountain. Anything that calmed her mind and broke the cycle of anxious thoughts.
- The Body Scan: She would quickly scan her body, noticing where she was holding tension. Her jaw. Her shoulders. Her stomach. And she would consciously release that tension.
- The Gratitude Moment: She would think of one thing she was grateful for. A simple pleasure. A kind gesture. A small victory. Shifting her attention, even for a few seconds, helped to disrupt the negative thought patterns.

She discovered that the 60-Second Stress Buster wasn't a one-size-fits-all solution. It was a flexible tool, a collection of techniques that she could adapt to different situations.

The key was to have it ready. To use it proactively, before the stress spiraled out of control.

It became her secret weapon. Her go-to defense against the daily onslaught.

She started to teach it to others. Her colleagues. Her friends. Even her sister, Brenda (who, surprisingly, seemed to benefit from it).

She realized that she wasn't alone in her struggle. Everyone was looking for ways to cope with the relentless pressure of modern life.

And the 60-Second Stress Buster, with its simplicity and effectiveness, was a lifeline.

It wasn't a magic bullet. It didn't eliminate stress entirely. But it gave her – and others – a fighting chance.

It gave them the power to choose. The power to respond, rather than react. The power to reclaim their lives, one minute at a time.

The city still roared. The demands still piled up. But Billie was no longer a victim of her circumstances.

She was a warrior. Equipped with a simple, but powerful weapon. The 60-Second Stress Buster.

And she was ready for the fight.

Chapter 5: Time Bandit Exposed

Billie stared at the screen. Hours. Gone. Vanished into the digital ether.

She'd sat down at her computer that morning with the best of intentions. A mountain of work loomed, Project Phoenix chief among them, but she was armed. She had her 60-Second Stress Buster. She had her Trigger Point list. She was ready.

Or so she thought.

Now, it was late afternoon. The mountain of work remained. And Billie felt like she'd been run over by a truck.

Where had the time gone?

She opened her browser history. A digital trail of breadcrumbs leading to... nowhere.

- Email. Hours. Endless emails. Reading them. Responding to them. Deleting them. A black hole of productivity.
- Social media. A quick check turned into a thirty-minute scroll. Cat videos. Political rants. Friends' vacation photos. A time vortex disguised as entertainment.
- News websites. The latest crisis. The breaking scandal. The doom and gloom. Each click a tiny hit of adrenaline, followed by a lingering sense of unease.
- Online shopping. Just browsing. A few minutes here, a few minutes there. Suddenly, an hour was gone, and she was the proud owner of a pair of shoes she didn't need.

The realization hit her like a punch to the gut. The Time Bandit. It wasn't some shadowy figure lurking in the dark. It was her.

She was the one stealing her own time. Piece by piece. Minute by minute.

She thought about her Trigger Point list. The Unrealistic Deadline. The Perfection Trap. The Information Overload. They were all connected.

The Unrealistic Deadline made her feel pressured, which led to the Perfection Trap, which made her procrastinate, which led to... the Time Bandit.

She was seeking escape. A temporary reprieve from the stress. And she was finding it in the digital abyss.

But the escape was an illusion. The more time she wasted, the more stressed she became. It was a vicious cycle.

She had to break it.

She decided to conduct an experiment. A time audit.

For one week, she would track her time. Every minute. Every activity. No exceptions.

She used a simple time-tracking app on her phone. It was tedious. It was eye-opening. It was terrifying.

The results were shocking.

- Email: 3 hours per day.
- Social media: 2 hours per day.
- News websites: 1 hour per day.
- Online shopping: 30 minutes per day.

- Meetings (many unproductive): 2 hours per day.
- Actual work on her Project: 2 hours per day.

Two hours. That's all she was spending on the most critical project. The project that was causing her the most stress.

She felt a surge of anger. At herself. For letting this happen. For being so easily distracted. For allowing her time to be stolen.

But anger wasn't productive. She needed a plan.

She needed to fight back.

She identified the Time Bandit's favorite tactics.

- The Seductive Siren: Social media. The endless scroll. The dopamine hits.
- The Urgent Imposter: Email. Every notification, every message, felt like a crisis.
- The Information Black Hole: News websites. The constant barrage of negativity.
- The Shiny Object Syndrome: Online Shopping. The allure of something new, something better.

She created a counter-strategy. A Time Bandit Busting Protocol.

- Email Lockdown: She set specific times to check email – three times a day, and only for a set period. She turned off notifications. She unsubscribed from unnecessary lists.
- Social Media Curfew: She limited herself to 30 minutes of social media per day, and only during her lunch break. She used a timer. She unfollowed accounts that triggered negative emotions.
- News Diet: She restricted her news intake to once a day, and only from reliable sources. She avoided clickbait headlines and doom-scrolling.
- Shopping Freeze: She unsubscribed from marketing emails from online retailers. She made a rule: no impulse purchases.
- Meeting Makeover: She started scheduling shorter, more focused meetings. She set agendas. She declined unnecessary invitations.

It wasn't easy. The Time Bandit fought back. The urge to check her phone, to scroll through social media, to click on that tempting headline was strong.

But Billie was stronger.

She used her 60-Second Stress Buster. She reminded herself of her goals. She was happy with the feeling of accomplishment when she actually made progress on her project.

Slowly, gradually, she started to reclaim her time.

She discovered the power of time blocking. She scheduled specific blocks of time for specific tasks. And she treated those blocks as sacred.

She learned to say "no" to distractions. To protect her time like a precious resource.

The results were dramatic.

Her stress levels decreased. Her productivity soared. She had more time for work, for her friends, for herself.

She started to feel... lighter. More in control. More alive.

The Time Bandit was exposed. Its power was diminished.

Billie had won a major victory in the war against stress.

She had reclaimed her time. And she was ready to use it wisely.

LESS STRESS: MORE YES

Chapter 6: the Power of "No"

The invitation arrived via email. Subject: URGENT: Volunteer Opportunity - Charity Gala Committee.

Billie's finger hovered over the "delete" button. A familiar feeling washed over her. Dread.

It wasn't the charity. It was a good cause. But the thought of another commitment, another demand on her already stretched time and energy, sent a shiver of anxiety down her spine.

She thought about the Time Bandit. How she'd clawed back those stolen hours. How she was finally starting to feel like she had some breathing room.

And now, this.

She knew what Julian would say. "It's for a good cause, Billie. Great networking opportunity."

Guilt. That was the weapon. The guilt trip. It wrapped around her like a constricting vine, whispering doubts and obligations.

You should do it. It's the right thing to do. You're a good person, aren't you?

She closed her eyes. Three deep breaths. The 60-Second Stress Buster. It helped, a little. But the guilt lingered.

She thought about her Trigger Point list. The Perfection Trap. The Guilt Trip. They were a deadly combination.

She wanted to be a good person. A helpful person. But at what cost?

She opened her email again. The invitation stared back at her.

She had a choice.

She could say "yes." Succumb to the guilt. Add another layer of stress to her already overflowing plate.

Or she could say "no."

The word hung in the air, small but powerful. A two-letter declaration of independence.

But how?

Saying "no" wasn't easy. It felt... wrong. Selfish.

She decided to do some research. She Googled "how to say no without feeling guilty." The internet, as always, had answers.

She found articles, blog posts, even videos. But most of them felt... weak. Apologetic.

"I'm so sorry, but I'm really busy right now..."

"I wish I could, but..."

Excuses. Explanations. Begging for forgiveness.

That wasn't her style. She needed something stronger. Something more... direct.

She thought about Mark. His bluntness. His unapologetic approach to getting what he wanted.

She didn't want to be like Mark. But she admired his ability to set boundaries.

She realized that saying "no" wasn't about being selfish. It was about being strategic. It was about protecting her time and energy so she could concentrate on what truly mattered.

It was about saying "yes" to herself.

She crafted her response.

Subject: Re: Volunteer Opportunity – Charity Gala Committee

Dear [Organizer Name],

Thank you for the invitation. I appreciate the opportunity to support such a worthy cause.

However, due to my current commitments, I am unable to participate at this time.

I wish you all the best with the gala.

Sincerely,

Billie [Last Name]

That was it. No excuses. No explanations. Just a simple, direct "no."

She hesitated for a moment. Her finger hovered over the "send" button.

The guilt gnawed at her. But she took another deep breath. She remembered her Time Bandit Busting Protocol. She remembered how much better she felt when she was in control of her time.

She clicked "send."

The email was gone.

And... nothing happened.

The world didn't end. The sky didn't fall. She didn't burst into flames.

She felt... relieved.

A weight had lifted off her shoulders. A small victory, but a significant one.

She had said "no." And she had survived.

She started to practice.

A friend invited her to a late-night networking event. "No, thank you," she said, politely but firmly.

A colleague asked her to take on an extra project. "I'm at capacity right now," she replied, without apology.

Her sister, Brenda, called, wanting to vent about her latest drama. "I only have a few minutes to talk," Billie said, setting a clear boundary.

It wasn't easy. People pushed back. They tried to guilt-trip her. They questioned her motives.

But Billie stood her ground. She remembered why she was doing this. She was reclaiming her life. She was saying "yes" to herself.

She discovered that saying "no" wasn't about being negative. It was about being positive.

It was about making conscious choices about how she wanted to spend her time and energy.

It was about prioritizing her well-being.

It was about creating space for the things that truly mattered.

Her relationships improved. People started to respect her boundaries. They realized that her "no" wasn't personal; it was a reflection of her priorities.

Her work improved. She was more focused, more productive, because she wasn't constantly drained by unnecessary commitments.

Her stress levels decreased. She felt more in control of her life.

The power of "no." It was a game-changer.

It wasn't always easy. But it was always worth it.

A quiet wisdom settled over Billie.

Sometimes, the most powerful thing you can say is "no."

And when you do, you're saying "yes" to yourself.

Part 2: Reclaiming Your Yes

LESS STRESS: MORE YES

Chapter 7: the "Yes" Inventory

Billie sat at her kitchen table, a steaming mug of herbal tea in front of her. The apartment was quiet, a stark contrast to the usual chaos of her life.

She had a new list in front of her. Not a list of triggers. Not a list of tasks. This was a different kind of inventory. A "Yes" Inventory.

For so long, her life had been defined by "no." No to social events. No to new projects. No to anything that threatened to add more stress to her already overflowing plate.

But what about "yes"?

What about the things that actually brought her joy? What about the activities that made her feel alive, energized, and fulfilled?

She realized she'd lost touch with them. Somewhere along the way, in the relentless pursuit of productivity and the constant battle against stress, she'd forgotten what it felt like to simply... enjoy life.

She stared at the blank page. It felt daunting. Like trying to remember a forgotten language.

What did she enjoy?

It wasn't as easy a question as she thought.

She started to brainstorm. She wrote down anything that came to mind, without judgment, without filtering.

- Reading. Not work-related articles or self-help books. Just good old-fashioned fiction. Stories that transported her to other worlds.
- Hiking. The feeling of being outdoors, surrounded by nature. The challenge of the climb. The breathtaking view from the top.
- Painting. She hadn't picked up a brush in years. But she remembered the feeling of

losing herself in the colors, the textures, the creative process.
- Laughter. Spending time with people who made her laugh until her sides hurt. The pure, unadulterated joy of shared humor.
- Live music. The energy of the crowd, the passion of the musicians, the feeling of being swept away by the rhythm.
- Cooking. Not just chucking together a quick meal. But actually experimenting with new recipes, savoring the flavors, sharing the experience with others.
- Learning. The thrill of discovering something new, expanding her knowledge, challenging her mind.

The list grew. It wasn't the works, but it was a start.

She looked at it, surprised. There were things on there she hadn't thought about in years. Things she used to love, things that used to define her.

Where had they gone?

The Time Bandit, she realized. And the Guilt Trip. They had conspired to steal her joy, to convince her that those things were frivolous, a waste of time.

But they weren't. They were essential. They were the fuel that kept her going. They were the reason she was fighting against stress in the first place.

She decided to take action.

She scheduled time for reading. She joined a hiking group. She signed up for a painting class. She made plans to see a live band with friends. She started experimenting with new recipes in the kitchen. She enrolled in an online course on a subject that had always fascinated her.

It wasn't easy, at first. It felt strange, even a little selfish, to prioritize these things.

The Guilt Trip tried to creep back in. You should be working. You should be catching up on emails. You should be doing something more productive.

But Billie pushed back. She used her 60-Second Stress Buster. She reminded herself of her "no" boundaries. She found joy in the positive feelings these activities brought her.

And slowly, gradually, something amazing happened.

She started to feel... happier.

The stress didn't disappear completely. But it became more manageable.

She had something to look forward to. Something to balance out the demands and pressures of work.

She discovered that the more she said "yes" to the things she enjoyed, the more energy she had for everything else.

Her work improved. She was more creative, more centered, more resilient.

Her relationships improved. She was more present, more engaged, more fun to be around.

Her stress levels decreased. She felt more balanced, more fulfilled, more alive.

It was a revelation.

It wasn't just about making a list. It was about making a commitment. A commitment to herself. A commitment to her joy.

It was about remembering who she was, what she loved, what made her heart sing.

It was about saying "yes" to life, in all its messy, beautiful, wonderful complexity.

Billie walked away wiser than before.

Life wasn't just about fighting against stress. It was also about fighting for joy.

And the "Yes" Inventory was her map, her guide, her compass on that journey.

Chapter 8: Micro-Adventures

The email pinged. It wasn't work. It wasn't a demand. It was... an invitation.

"Escape Room Challenge this Saturday! Anyone interested?"

Billie almost deleted it. Saturday. Another day. Another potential source of stress. Another opportunity to say "no."

But then, she remembered her "Yes" Inventory. Laughter. Excitement. Trying new things.

An escape room. It wasn't something she would normally do. It was... adventurous. A little bit scary. And definitely outside her comfort zone.

A micro-adventure.

The term popped into her head. She'd read about it somewhere. The idea of injecting small doses of adventure into everyday life. Not skydiving or climbing Mount Everest, but something that pushed her boundaries, even just a little.

She hesitated. The Guilt Trip started its familiar whisper campaign. You have work to do. You should be catching up on chores. You don't have time for this.

But Billie was getting better at recognizing the Guilt Trip. She knew its tricks. She knew its lies.

She thought about the past few weeks. How much better she'd been feeling. How much more alive she was since she started saying "yes" to the things she enjoyed.

An escape room. It was only a couple of hours. It was a chance to have fun, to laugh, to challenge herself.

She typed a response.

"I'm in!"

The word felt... liberating.

Saturday arrived. Billie found herself standing in front of a nondescript building in an unfamiliar part of town. The sign outside read, "Mind Games Escape Room."

She felt a flutter of nerves. What had she gotten herself into?

Inside, she met the others. A mix of friends and strangers. They were all smiling, excited. The energy was infectious.

The game began. The door slammed shut. They were locked in a room filled with puzzles, clues, and hidden messages.

The clock started ticking.

Billie felt a surge of adrenaline. This wasn't work. This wasn't stress. This was... fun.

They worked together, solving riddles, cracking codes, searching for clues. Billie found herself laughing, shouting, high-fiving strangers.

For a few hours, she forgot about the project. She forgot about deadlines. She forgot about the weight of the world.

She was just... present. In the moment. Enjoying the challenge, the camaraderie, the sheer thrill of the unknown.

They escaped with minutes to spare.

Billie emerged from the escape room, buzzing with energy. She felt... exhilarated. Alive.

It was just an escape room. A few hours of her life. But it had made a difference.

It had reminded her that life wasn't just about surviving. It was about thriving. It was about seeking out new experiences, even small ones.

It was about embracing the unexpected.

She started to look for other micro-adventures.

She tried a new restaurant. She took a different route home from work. She went to a poetry slam. She signed up for Tango lessons.

Each one was small. Each one was manageable. But each one added a spark of excitement, a touch of novelty, to her daily routine.

She discovered that micro-adventures weren't just about having fun. They were also a powerful stress reliever.

They broke the monotony of her routine. They forced her to be present. They reminded her that life was full of possibilities.

They also made her more resilient. When she faced challenges at work, she remembered the feeling of overcoming obstacles in the escape room. She remembered that she was capable of more than she thought.

Micro-adventures became a regular part of her life. She actually put them on her calendar, just like she would for work.

They weren't just a way to avoid her chores or work. They were something she needed to do to take care of herself.

It was her way of saying "Sure, why not?" to enjoying life, one small adventure at a time.

That day, Billie understood something important.

You don't have to climb a mountain to have an adventure. Sometimes, the greatest adventures are the ones you find in your own backyard.

LESS STRESS: MORE YES

Chapter 9: the Done List Revolution

Billie stared at her to-do list. It was a monster. A sprawling, ever-growing pile of tasks, deadlines, and obligations.

- Project Phoenix: Presentation Prep
- Client Meeting: Freedthinkers.com
- Email: Respond to 37 Unread Messages
- Groceries
- Laundry
- Call Mom
- Schedule Dentist Appointment

- Research Norway Proposal
- Write Blog Post
- Pick up Dry Cleaning

The sheer volume of it was enough to trigger a panic attack. She felt like she was drowning in a sea of tasks, with no hope of ever reaching the shore.

She'd been trying to be more organized, more efficient. She'd used different apps, different systems, different planners. But the to-do list always won. It always seemed to multiply faster than she could cross things off.

She felt a familiar wave of stress wash over her. The pressure of all these unfinished tasks, the constant feeling of being behind, was overwhelming.

She remembered a conversation she'd had with a mentor, years ago. He'd said, "Focus on what you've done, not just what you have to do."

At the time, it had sounded like a nice sentiment. But now, it felt like a revelation.

What if she focused on her accomplishments instead of her obligations? What if she created a "done" list?

The idea was radical, almost rebellious. It went against everything she'd been taught about productivity and time management.

But Billie was tired of feeling like a failure. She was tired of stressing about what she hadn't done. She wanted to celebrate her successes, no matter how small.

She grabbed a new notebook and a pen. She titled the first page, "Done List."

Then, she started to write.

- Woke up before 7 AM.
- Made a healthy breakfast.
- Did 2 hours of focused work on Project Phoenix.
- Replied to 14 emails.
- Took a 15-minute walk during lunch.
- Had a productive meeting with a colleague.
- Made dinner.
- Read for 30 minutes.
- Went to bed before 11 PM.

She looked at the list. It wasn't a list of major achievements. It was a list of everyday actions. But it felt... good.

She had actually accomplished something. She had moved through her day, completing tasks, making progress.

The to-do list was still there, looming in the background. But the done list gave her a sense of momentum, a feeling of control.

She started to track her done list every day. She added items as she completed them, no matter how small.

- Sent a difficult email.
- Paid a bill.
- Made someone laugh.
- Learned something new.
- Said "no" to an unnecessary request.
- Practiced the 60-Second Stress Buster.
- Went to a Tango class.

The done list became a source of motivation. It reminded her that she was capable, that she was making progress, that she was moving in the right direction.

It also helped her to identify her strengths and her priorities. She noticed that she consistently completed tasks related to her work and her self-care. Those were the areas where she was the most effective.

The to-do list didn't disappear. But it lost its power. It was no longer a source of stress, but a guide.

Billie started to use her done list to plan her to-do list. She looked at what she had accomplished in the past and used that information to set realistic goals for the future.

She also started to reward herself for completing tasks. Not with extravagant gifts, but with small pleasures. A cup of tea. A few minutes of quiet time. A walk in the park.

The done list revolution had begun.

Billie wouldn't forget what life taught her.

Focusing on your accomplishments is just as important as focusing on your obligations.

The done list is a powerful tool for building momentum, reducing stress, and celebrating your successes.

It's a way of saying "yes" to yourself, one small victory at a time.

LESS STRESS: MORE YES

Chapter 10: Energy Vampires? Stake Them!

Billie walked into the coffee shop. It was her usual haunt, a place of relative calm amidst the city's chaos. But today, the calm was shattered.

Brenda. Her sister.

Billie spotted her in the corner, surrounded by a swirling vortex of negativity. Brenda was holding court, her face a mask of perpetual woe.

Billie felt a familiar sinking feeling. This. This was an Energy Vampire convention.

Brenda had a gift. A gift for sucking the life out of any room, any conversation, any human being unfortunate enough to cross her path.

It wasn't intentional, Billie knew. Brenda wasn't a bad person. She was just... a black hole of negativity. A bottomless pit of complaints and problems. A drama queen.

Every conversation with Brenda left Billie feeling drained, exhausted, and emotionally hungover. It was like she'd been plugged into a power socket, and all her energy had been siphoned away.

Billie sat down, bracing herself.

"You won't believe what happened to me," Brenda began, her voice dripping with self-pity. "My boss... he's such a..."

And she was off. A litany of grievances, a symphony of suffering. Billie listened, nodding occasionally, trying to look interested.

But inside, her energy was draining. Her optimism was fading. Her patience was wearing thin.

She thought about her "Yes" Inventory. Laughter. Joy. Connection. Brenda was the opposite of all those things.

She thought about her Time Bandit Busting Protocol. She was so careful about protecting her time from digital distractions. But what about this? This human distraction, this emotional drain?

She realized something. Energy Vampires were real. They weren't supernatural creatures, but they were just as dangerous. They preyed on your empathy, your good nature, your willingness to listen. And they left you feeling depleted and defeated.

Brenda finally paused for breath. "...and then, he said... can you believe it?"

Billie took a deep breath. The 60-Second Stress Buster. She needed it now.

She decided to try a new tactic. A radical approach.

"Brenda," she said. "I hear what you're saying. And I'm sorry you're going through a tough time. But I'm feeling really drained right now, and I need to conserve my energy. Can we talk about something else?"

Brenda stared at her, stunned. "What? What do you mean?"

Billie held her gaze. "I mean, I'm happy to support you. But I need to set some boundaries. I can't listen to a non-stop stream of negativity without it affecting me. Can we talk about something positive, or maybe do something else?"

It was like she'd spoken a foreign language. Brenda blinked, confused. "But... but my problems..."

"Your problems are valid," Billie said. "But so are my needs. I need to protect my energy."

The conversation shifted. It wasn't easy. Brenda kept trying to steer it back to her moans and groans. But Billie gently, firmly, redirected her.

They ended up talking about Brenda's new hobby, a pottery class she'd been taking. For the first time in years, Billie saw a spark of genuine enthusiasm in her sister's eyes.

Billie left the coffee shop feeling... different. Not drained. Not exhausted. But... energized.

She had staked an Energy Vampire.

It wasn't about cutting Brenda out of her life. It was about setting boundaries. It was about protecting her own energy.

She realized that Brenda wasn't the only Energy Vampire in her life. There were others.

- Mark, her boss. His constant demands, his relentless pressure, his inability to acknowledge her accomplishments.
- A colleague who always complained about everything, spreading negativity like a virus.
- A friend who constantly borrowed money and never paid it back.
- A family member who always criticized her choices, making her feel inadequate.

Billie started to identify them. She made a list. Her own personal rogues' gallery of Energy Vampires.

And she started to take action.

With Mark, she set clear boundaries about her work hours and her workload. She started documenting her accomplishments, so he couldn't dismiss them.

With the complaining colleague, she limited her interactions and politely changed the subject whenever the negativity started flowing.

With the friend who borrowed money, she said "no" firmly and consistently.

With the critical family member, she limited her contact and stopped seeking their approval.

It wasn't easy. People resisted. They tried to guilt-trip her. They accused her of being selfish.

But Billie stood her ground. She remembered how much better she felt when she protected her energy.

A hard truth finally clicked for Billie.

You have the right to protect your energy. You don't have to be a martyr. You don't have to sacrifice your well-being for others.

Setting boundaries isn't selfish; it's a survival skill.

And sometimes, the most loving thing you can do for yourself – and for others – is to stake those Energy Vampires and get your life back.

Chapter 11: The Art of Delegation

Billie sat at her desk, surrounded by a mountain of paperworkl.

The presentation loomed, a deadline monster breathing down her neck. She felt the pressure building, the tightness in her chest, the urge to reach for the 60-Second Stress Buster.

She looked at her to-do list. It was a disaster. A tangled web of tasks, many of which she knew, deep down, she didn't have to do herself.

She thought about delegation. The word felt... Wierd. Alien. Like a concept from another planet.

Delegation wasn't her strong suit. She was a control freak. A perfectionist. She liked things done a certain way. Her way.

The thought of handing over a task to someone else, of relinquishing control, filled her with anxiety. What if they messed it up? What if they didn't do it right? What if it ended up creating more work for her?

She'd tried delegating before. With mixed results. A colleague had dropped the ball on a crucial detail. An assistant had misinterpreted her instructions. Each experience had reinforced her belief that it was easier just to do it herself.

But she was drowning. She was burning out. She couldn't keep going like this.

She remembered a piece of advice she'd read: "If you want to go fast, go alone. If you want to go far, go together."

She wanted to go far. She wanted to build a sustainable, stress-free life. And that meant learning to delegate.

She decided to try a different approach. A more strategic, more deliberate approach.

She started by analyzing her to-do list. She identified the tasks that were truly essential for her to do herself, the tasks that required her unique skills and expertise.

Then, she identified the tasks that could be delegated. The tasks that were routine, administrative, or that could be done by someone else with the right training and guidance.

She categorized them.

- Delegate Immediately: Tasks that were urgent but not critical, that could be handed off right away.
- Delegate with Training: Tasks that required some training or instruction, but that could be delegated in the near future.
- Delegate Eventually: Tasks that were important but not urgent, that could be delegated over time as she built trust and confidence in her team.
- Do Not Delegate: Tasks that were critical and required her personal attention.

She identified potential delegates. Her assistant, who was eager to take on more responsibility. A colleague who had expertise in a certain area. Even some tasks she could outsource to freelancers.

She started small. She delegated a few simple tasks to her assistant. She provided clear instructions, set deadlines, and offered support.

To her surprise, her assistant did a great job. The tasks were completed efficiently and accurately. And Billie had freed up some time and energy.

She felt a glimmer of hope. Maybe delegation wasn't so bad after all.

She gradually delegated more tasks, with increasing confidence. She learned to trust her team, to let go of control, to focus on the bigger picture.

She also learned to communicate effectively. She provided clear instructions, set expectations, and gave feedback. She learned to empower her team, to give them autonomy, to recognize their contributions.

Delegation wasn't just about offloading tasks. It was about building a team. It was about creating a system. It was about leveraging the skills and talents of others.

It wasn't always easy. There were setbacks. There were mistakes. But Billie learned from them. She adjusted her approach. She improved her communication.

Slowly, gradually, she became a master delegator.

Her stress levels decreased. Her productivity soared. She had more time for the things that truly mattered: her work, her friends, her self-care.

She discovered that delegation wasn't a sign of weakness. It was a sign of strength.

It was a way of saying "yes" to efficiency, "yes" to collaboration, and "yes" to a more balanced and fulfilling life.

That moment left Billie with a lasting lesson.

You don't have to do everything yourself. You can't do everything yourself.

The art of delegation is essential for managing stress, maximizing productivity, and building a strong team.

And sometimes, the best way to get things done is to let go and let others help you.

LESS STRESS: MORE YES

Part 3: Building a Stress-Resistant Life

LESS STRESS: MORE YES

Chapter 12: Sleep Is Your Superpower

Billie stared at the ceiling. 3:17 AM. Again.

The numbers on her digital clock glowed with a brooding intensity, mocking her. Sleep. That elusive, magical state seemed to have abandoned her.

She'd tried everything. Warm milk. Chamomile tea. White noise. Meditation apps. Counting sheep (which, she'd discovered, was surprisingly stressful).

Nothing worked.

She tossed and turned, her mind racing, replaying the day's events, anticipating tomorrow's stuff, a relentless hamster wheel of anxious thoughts.

She felt like a zombie. Foggy-headed, irritable, and perpetually exhausted. Her productivity was plummeting. Her stress levels were soaring. And her health... well, her health was starting to show the strain.

Dark circles under her eyes. Headaches that throbbed like a jackhammer. A constant feeling of being on edge, ready to snap at any moment.

She knew, intellectually, that sleep was important. She'd read the articles, the studies, the expert advice. But knowing and experiencing were two very different things.

For her, sleep wasn't a luxury. It was a battlefield. A nightly struggle against insomnia, anxiety, and the relentless demands of her life.

She thought about her "Yes" Inventory. Energy. Vitality. Feeling good. Sleep was the foundation of all those things. Without it, she was running on empty.

She decided to take a more aggressive approach. A sleep intervention.

She consulted a sleep specialist. A practical doctor who didn't mince words.

"You're sleep-deprived," he told her bluntly. "Your body is in a constant state of stress. You need to make sleep a priority, not an afterthought."

He gave her a list of instructions. Not suggestions. Instructions.

- The Sleep Sanctuary: Her bedroom was to become a sacred space, dedicated to sleep. Dark, quiet, and cool. No screens. No work. No clutter.
- The Ritual: A consistent bedtime routine. A warm bath. Gentle stretching. Reading an actual book (not an e-reader).
- The Digital Sunset: All screens off at least an hour before bed. No phones. No laptops. No tablets.
- The Caffeine Cutoff: No caffeine after noon. Not even a sneaky cup of tea.
- The Consistency Rule: Same bedtime and wake-up time, even on weekends. No more sleeping in.
- The Worry Window: A designated time during the day to address her worries, rather than letting them fester at night.

It was a radical overhaul of her lifestyle. It felt... restrictive. But Billie was desperate. She was willing to try anything.

She transformed her bedroom into a sleep sanctuary. She invested in blackout curtains, a white noise machine, and a comfortable mattress.

She established a bedtime ritual. A warm bath, a few gentle yoga stretches, and a chapter of a relaxing novel.

She enforced the digital sunset. It was painful at first. The urge to check her phone was almost unbearable. But she resisted.

She stuck to the caffeine cutoff. She discovered herbal teas and the joy of being caffeine-free in the afternoon.

She followed the consistency rule. It was tough on weekends, but she kept at it.

She implemented the worry window. She scheduled 30 minutes each day to address her concerns, to make plans, to take action. And then, she let them go.

Slowly, gradually, something amazing happened.

She started to sleep.

Not perfectly. Not every night. But more consistently. More deeply. More restoratively.

She woke up feeling... refreshed. Energized. Ready to face the day.

Her productivity soared. Her stress levels decreased. Her mood improved.

She discovered that sleep wasn't a luxury. It was a superpower.

It wasn't just about feeling rested. It was about boosting her immune system, improving her memory, regulating her emotions, and enhancing her creativity.

It was about giving her body and her mind the time they needed to repair, to recharge, to thrive.

Billie came to see things in a new light.

Sleep isn't a weakness. It's a strength.

Prioritizing sleep is essential for managing stress, improving your health, and unlocking your full potential.

And sometimes, the most productive thing you can do is... nothing. Just close your eyes and let your body do its magic.

Chapter 13: Fuel Your Fire

Billie stood in her kitchen, staring into the refrigerator. It wasn't a pretty sight.

Takeout containers. Leftovers that had seen better days. A wilted head of lettuce. A lone, forgotten carrot.

Her diet. It was a disaster. A haphazard collection of convenience foods and unhealthy choices, driven by stress, fueled by exhaustion, and devoid of any semblance of nutritional value.

She knew she wasn't alone. In the fast-paced, high-pressure world she lived in, healthy eating often took a backseat. It was easier, quicker, and seemingly cheaper to grab a burger, order pizza, or microwave a frozen meal.

But she was starting to feel the consequences. Her energy levels were all over the place. Her mood was unpredictable. Her body felt sluggish and heavy.

Her current diet was the opposite of all those things. It was draining her fire, not fueling it.

She decided to take action. A nutritional intervention.

She consulted a nutritionist. A practical woman who didn't preach or judge.

"You don't need to become a vegan overnight," she told Billie. "Just make small, sustainable changes. Concentrate on adding more good stuff, rather than restricting everything bad."

She gave Billie a simple framework.

- The 80/20 Rule: Aim to eat healthy, whole foods 80% of the time. Allow for some flexibility and indulgence 20% of the time.
- The Rainbow Plate: Fill your plate with a variety of colorful fruits and vegetables. Each color provides different nutrients.

- The Hydration Habit: Drink plenty of water during the day. Dehydration can lead to fatigue, headaches, and other stress-related symptoms.
- The Mindful Meal: Eat slowly, without distractions. Savor the flavors, textures, and aromas of your food.
- The Sugar Slash: Reduce your intake of added sugar. It can cause energy crashes, mood swings, and weight gain.
- The Processed Food Purge: Minimize your consumption of highly processed foods, which are often loaded with unhealthy fats, sugar, and sodium.

It wasn't a radical diet. It was a common-sense approach to eating. But it required a shift in mindset, a commitment to taking her health seriously.

Billie started small. She added a green smoothie to her breakfast routine. She packed healthy snacks for work. She started cooking more meals at home.

She experimented with new recipes, incorporating more fruits, vegetables, and whole grains into her diet. She discovered the joy of cooking, the satisfaction of nourishing her body with wholesome foods.

She drank more water. She carried a reusable water bottle with her everywhere she went. She noticed that she felt more energized and less prone to headaches.

She practiced mindful eating. She turned off her phone during meals. She sensed the taste, smell, and texture of her food. She found that she ate less and enjoyed her meals more.

She reduced her sugar intake. She switched to natural sweeteners like honey and maple syrup. She started reading food labels, becoming more aware of hidden sugars.

She minimized her consumption of processed foods. She started making her own salad dressings, snacks, and sauces. She discovered that whole, unprocessed foods tasted better and made her feel better.

Slowly, gradually, something amazing happened.

Her energy levels stabilized. She no longer experienced the afternoon slump or the late-night cravings.

Her mood improved. She felt more balanced, more even-keeled, less prone to irritability and anxiety.

Her body felt lighter, stronger, and more vibrant. She noticed that her clothes fit better and that she had more stamina.

She discovered that food wasn't just fuel. It was medicine.

It wasn't just about surviving. It was about thriving.

It was about giving her body the nutrients it needed to function at its best, to fight off stress, and to support her overall well-being.

Billie got the kind of education no school could offer.

You can't outrun a bad diet.

Fueling your body with healthy, whole foods is essential for managing stress, improving your health, and living a vibrant life.

And sometimes, the most powerful thing you can do for yourself is to nourish your body from the inside out.

LESS STRESS: MORE YES

Chapter 14: Movement as Medicine

Billie glanced at her gym membership card. It was gathering dust.

She'd joined with the best of intentions. New year, new you, right? But the reality of her life - the long hours, the constant pressure, the sheer exhaustion - had conspired against her. The gym had become another source of stress, another item on her ever-growing to-do list.

She knew she should exercise. Everyone said so. Doctors, experts, even her friends. But the thought of pounding the treadmill, lifting weights, or slogging through a grueling spin class filled her with dread.

She wasn't a gym person. She wasn't an athlete. She wasn't even particularly... coordinated.

But she was starting to feel the effects of her sedentary lifestyle. Stiffness. Aches. Low energy. And a general feeling of being... disconnected from her body.

She thought about her "Yes" Inventory. Energy. Vitality. Feeling good. Movement was essential for all those things. But how could she incorporate it into her life without adding more stress?

She decided to take a different approach. A movement intervention.

She consulted a physical therapist. A pragmatic, down-to-earth woman who understood the challenges of a busy life.

"You don't need to train for a marathon," she told Billie. "Just move your body. Find something you enjoy. And make it a habit."

She gave Billie a simple framework.

- The 10-Minute Rule: Aim for at least 10 minutes of movement every day. It's less daunting than an hour-long workout, and it's surprisingly effective.

- The Joyful Movement: Choose activities you actually enjoy. If you hate running, don't run. If you love dancing, dance.
- The Body Scan: Pay attention to how your body feels during and after movement. Notice the sensations, the changes in energy, the release of tension.
- The Micro-Movements: Incorporate small movements throughout the day. Take the stairs instead of the elevator. Walk during your lunch break. Stretch at your desk.
- The Social Sweat: Exercise with a friend, a family member, or a group. It's more fun and more motivating.
- The Outdoor Option: Move your body outdoors whenever possible. Nature has a calming effect on the mind and body.

It wasn't a rigid exercise plan. It was a flexible, adaptable approach to incorporating movement into her life.

Billie started small. She began with 10-minute walks during her lunch break. She discovered a park near work with a walking trail. The fresh air and the change of scenery were a welcome break from the office.

She tried a Tango class. It was intimidating at first, but she soon found herself laughing, moving, and enjoying the music. She realized that exercise didn't have to be a chore; it could be fun.

She incorporated micro-movements into her workday. She took the stairs instead of the elevator. She stood up and stretched every hour. She even started pacing during phone calls.

She invited a friend to join her for a weekend hike. They talked, laughed, and enjoyed the beautiful scenery. The social aspect made the movement even more enjoyable.

She spent more time outdoors. She went for walks in the park, even on rainy days. She discovered that being in nature had a calming and restorative effect on her mind and body.

Slowly, gradually, something amazing happened.

Her energy levels increased. She felt more vibrant and less sluggish.

Her mood improved. She felt more balanced and less prone to stress and anxiety.

Her body felt stronger, more flexible, and more resilient. She noticed that her aches and pains started to subside.

She discovered that movement wasn't just about physical health. It was medicine for her mind and her soul.

It wasn't just about surviving. It was about thriving.

It was about connecting with her body, releasing tension, and experiencing the joy of being alive.

Billie realized something she'd never noticed before.

You don't have to be an athlete to benefit from movement.

Incorporating small amounts of joyful movement into your daily life is essential for managing stress, improving your health, and feeling your best.

And sometimes, the most powerful thing you can do for yourself is to simply... move.

# LESS STRESS: MORE YES

Chapter 15: the Mind Game Advantage

Billie sat in a quiet room, headphones on, listening to a voice. Not a demanding boss, not a complaining sister, but a calm, soothing voice.

"Imagine a peaceful place," the voice said. "A place where you feel safe, relaxed, and at ease..."

She was trying meditation.

Meditation wasn't on her radar - it seemed too far out, too New Age, and definitely not her thing.

But she was desperate. The stress of her life, even with all the changes she'd made, still lingered. It was like a stubborn shadow, always lurking in the background, ready to pounce.

She realized that she'd been working on changing her external circumstances – her work, her habits, her relationships. But she hadn't addressed the root of the problem: her mind.

Her mind was a battlefield. A constant barrage of thoughts, worries, and negative self-talk. It was like she had a committee of anxious gremlins living in her head, constantly chattering and creating chaos.

She thought about her "Yes" Inventory. Calmness. Focus. Resilience. Her current mind game was the opposite of all those things. She needed a new strategy.

She decided to take a mental intervention.

She consulted a mindfulness teacher. A practical, grounded woman who understood the skepticism of busy, modern people.

"Meditation isn't about emptying your mind," she told Billie. "It's about training your attention. It's about learning to observe your thoughts without getting carried away by them."

She gave Billie a simple framework.

- The Breath Focus: Start by sensing your breath. The sensation of the air entering and leaving your body. It's an anchor to the present moment.
- The Thought Observer: Notice your thoughts as they arise. Don't judge them, don't try to stop them. Just observe them, like clouds passing in the sky.
- The Body Awareness: Pay attention to the sensations in your body. Tension, relaxation, discomfort, ease. It helps you to connect with your physical self.
- The Kind Attention: Treat yourself with kindness and compassion. When your mind wanders (and it will), gently redirect it back to your breath, without self-criticism.
- The Daily Practice: Start with just 5 or 10 minutes of meditation each day. Consistency is more important than duration.
- The Mindful Moments: Incorporate mindfulness into your daily activities. Pay attention to the feeling of the water on your hands when you wash dishes, the taste of your

food when you eat, the sounds around you when you walk.

It wasn't about becoming a monk. It was about developing a skill, a mental muscle, that could help her navigate the challenges of her life with more calm and clarity.

Billie started small. She began with 5 minutes of guided meditation each morning. She sat in a quiet room, closed her eyes, and focused on her breath.

Her mind wandered. A lot. She got frustrated. She felt like she was doing it wrong.

But she stuck at it. She remembered the teacher's words: "Don't judge your thoughts. Just observe them."

Slowly, she started to notice a shift.

Her thoughts were still there, but they didn't have the same power over her. She could observe them without getting swept away by them.

She started to incorporate mindfulness into her daily activities. She paid attention to the feel of the keyboard as she typed, the warmth of the sun on her skin, the sound of her own footsteps as she walked.

She discovered that mindfulness wasn't just about sitting in silence. It was about being present in her life, fully engaged in each moment, without judgment or distraction.

She used mindfulness to manage stress. When she felt overwhelmed, she took a few deep breaths and focused on the sensations in her body. She noticed the tension in her shoulders, the tightness in her chest, and she consciously released it.

She used mindfulness to improve her attention. When her mind wandered during meetings, she gently redirected her concentration back to the speaker. She found that she was more present, more engaged, and more productive.

She used mindfulness to cultivate resilience. When she faced setbacks or challenges, she observed her thoughts and emotions without getting caught up in them. She reminded herself that setbacks were temporary, that she could learn from them, and that she could bounce back.

Gradually, something amazing happened.

Her stress levels decreased. She felt calmer, more centered, and less reactive.

Her concentration improved. She was more present, more efficient, and more creative.

Her resilience grew. She was better able to cope with challenges, to adapt to change, and to bounce back from adversity.

She discovered that her mind wasn't her enemy. It was a powerful tool, capable of great creativity and resilience.

It wasn't about eliminating her thoughts. It was about training them, directing them, and using them to her advantage.

Life pulled Billie aside and gave her a talking-to.

You can't always control your circumstances, but you can control your mind.

And sometimes, the most powerful thing you can do is to simply... pay attention.

Chapter 16: Digital Detox

Billie's phone buzzed. Again.

Email. Work. A client demanding an update. Another notification. Another interruption. Another demand on her already fragmented attention.

She felt a familiar wave of anxiety wash over her. The constant barrage of digital information, the relentless pinging and buzzing, the feeling of being perpetually connected and perpetually on call.

She thought about the Time Bandit. She'd fought hard to reclaim her time, to wrest it back from the clutches of digital distractions. But the distractions kept multiplying. The emails, the texts, the social media updates, the news alerts – they were a relentless tide, threatening to pull her under.

She thought about her "Yes" Inventory. Calmness. Focus. Presence. Her current digital habits were the antithesis of all those things. She needed a new strategy. An escape plan.

She decided to take a digital intervention.

She consulted a digital wellness expert. A no-nonsense woman who understood the allure of technology but also recognized its dark side.

"Technology isn't inherently bad," she told Billie. "It's how we use it. We need to develop a healthy relationship with our devices, a relationship based on intention, not addiction."

She gave Billie a simple framework.

- The Digital Sunset (Revisited): Extend the digital sunset. No screens for at least two hours before bed. The blue light emitted by screens interferes with sleep.
- The Notification Ninja: Tame the notifications. Turn off all non-essential notifications. Only allow notifications from people and apps that are truly important.

- The Intentional Check-In: Schedule specific times to check email and social media. Resist the urge to check constantly. Treat it like any other appointment.
- The App Audit: Review the apps on your phone and delete the ones that are time-wasters or that trigger negative emotions. Be ruthless.
- The Phone-Free Zones: Designate certain areas and times as phone-free zones. The bedroom. The dinner table. Family time.
- The Digital Sabbath: Take a complete break from technology for one day each week. A 24-hour period of unplugging and reconnecting with the real world.

It wasn't about abandoning technology altogether. It was about creating boundaries, developing healthy habits, and regaining control of her attention.

Billie started small. She extended her digital sunset. It was difficult at first. The urge to check her phone before bed was strong. But she replaced it with reading a physical book, taking a warm bath, and practicing a short meditation.

She tamed her notifications. She turned off all but the most essential alerts. The silence was... liberating. She found that she was less distracted.

She scheduled specific times to check email and social media. She resisted the urge to check constantly. She treated it like a chore, not a source of entertainment.

She conducted an app audit. She deleted several time-wasting apps from her phone. She felt a sense of relief, like she'd decluttered her digital life.

She designated phone-free zones. The bedroom became a sanctuary for sleep and intimacy. The dinner table became a place for conversation and connection.

She started taking a digital sabbath. It was the most challenging part. The first few Saturdays felt... empty. She didn't know what to do with herself. But she gradually rediscovered the joy of offline activities: reading, hiking, spending time with friends, exploring her city.

Slowly, gradually, something amazing happened.

Her sleep improved dramatically. She fell asleep faster, slept more deeply, and woke up feeling refreshed.

Her mind sharpened. She was more present in her conversations, more engaged in her work, and more creative in her thinking.

Her stress levels decreased. She felt calmer, more centered, and less reactive.

Her relationships deepened. She was more present with her loved ones, more connected to her community, and more attuned to the world around her.

She discovered that technology was a tool, not a master. She could use it on her terms, without letting it control her life.

It wasn't about escaping from the world. It was about escaping from the digital noise and reconnecting with what truly mattered: herself, her relationships, and the world around her.

Billie's perspective shifted, just a little—but forever.

You can't live a fully present life if you're constantly tethered to your devices.

A digital detox is essential for managing stress and reclaiming your time and attention.

And sometimes, the most powerful thing you can do is to simply... unplug.

LESS STRESS: MORE YES

Part 4: The More Yes Multiplier

LESS STRESS: MORE YES

Chapter 17: Embrace the Unexpected

Billie had a plan. A meticulously crafted, color-coded, time-blocked plan. Her life was a well-oiled machine, a symphony of productivity and self-care.

Or so she thought.

Then, the universe decided to throw her a curveball.

It started with a phone call. Not work. Not a client demanding an update. But her landlord.

"There's a burst pipe," he said. "Your apartment... it's flooded."

Flooded. The word hung in the air, a cold, wet reality. All her carefully laid plans, all her hard-won progress, threatened to be washed away.

Billie felt a familiar wave of panic. This wasn't in the plan. This was chaos. This was... unexpected.

She rushed home. The scene that greeted her was... biblical. Water everywhere. Soaked carpets. Damaged furniture. Her carefully organized life turned into a soggy mess.

She spent the next few days dealing with the aftermath. Insurance adjusters. Contractors. Replacing damaged items. Living in a temporary, cramped apartment.

It was stressful. It was disruptive. It was a complete disaster.

But as she navigated the chaos, something strange happened.

She started to... adapt.

She realized that she couldn't control everything. That life was unpredictable. That curveballs were inevitable.

She remembered her mindfulness practice. She concentrated on the present moment, on dealing with each challenge as it arose, without getting overwhelmed by the big picture.

She remembered her 60-Second Stress Buster. She used it frequently, to calm her anxiety and regain her composure.

She remembered her "Yes" Inventory. She found moments of joy and connection amidst the chaos, spending time with friends who offered support, finding humor in the absurdity of the situation.

She even discovered some unexpected benefits.

She decluttered her life. She got rid of things she didn't need. She realized how much stuff she'd accumulated, how much of it was just weighing her down.

She connected with her neighbors. She met people she'd never spoken to before, bonding over their shared experience of the flood. She discovered a sense of community she hadn't known existed.

She learned to be more flexible. She had to adjust her schedule, her plans, her expectations. She discovered that she was more adaptable than she thought.

Slowly, gradually, she started to see the flood not as a disaster, but as an opportunity.

An opportunity to declutter her life, to connect with her community, to learn to embrace the unexpected.

The flood eventually subsided. Her apartment was repaired. Life returned to normal.

But Billie was different.

She was less attached to her plans, less rigid in her expectations, more open to the surprises that life threw her way.

She discovered that the unexpected wasn't always bad. That sometimes, the best things in life happened when you least expected them.

She learned to embrace the chaos, to find the silver lining in every situation, to say "yes" to the unknown.

That experience carved a lesson deep into Billie's heart.

Life is unpredictable. You can't control everything.

Learning to embrace the unexpected is essential for managing stress, adapting to change, and living a more joyful and fulfilling life.

And sometimes, the best things happen when you least expect them.

LESS STRESS: MORE YES

Chapter 18: the Power of Connection

Billie sat at a table, surrounded by laughter. Not the forced, polite laughter of a work event, but the genuine, kind that only real friends could spark.

It was game night. A tradition she'd almost forgotten existed. A simple gathering of people, sharing food, playing games, and enjoying each other's company.

For so long, her life had been a solo mission. A relentless pursuit of productivity and self-improvement, fueled by her own determination and willpower. She'd become a master of self-reliance, a lone wolf navigating the urban jungle.

But she'd also become... isolated.

Her relationships had suffered. She'd canceled plans, declined invitations, prioritized work over people. She'd convinced herself that she was too busy, too stressed, too overwhelmed to invest in her friendships.

She thought about her "Yes" Inventory. Laughter. Joy. Connection. She'd been chasing the first two, but she'd neglected the third, the foundation upon which the others were built.

She realized that she wasn't an island. That she needed people. That she thrived on connection, on shared experiences, on the simple act of being with others.

She decided to take a relational intervention.

She consulted a relationship therapist. A warm, empathetic woman who understood the challenges of modern life and the importance of human connection.

"We are social creatures," she told Billie. "We are wired for connection. Isolation is a major stressor, a silent killer. We need to prioritize our relationships, not as a luxury, but as a necessity."

She gave Billie a simple framework.

- The Reach Out Rule: Reach out to at least one person each day. A text, a call, an email, a coffee date. Make it a habit.
- The Quality Time Quest: Schedule regular quality time with the people you care about. Put it on your calendar, just like any other important appointment.
- The Active Listener: When you're with someone, be fully present. Put your phone away, make eye contact, listen attentively, give feedback, and show genuine interest.
- The Vulnerability Venture: Don't be afraid to be vulnerable. Share your feelings, your struggles, your joys. Authenticity fosters deeper connection.
- The Appreciation Attitude: Express your appreciation for the people in your life. Tell them how much they mean to you. Show your gratitude.

- The Forgiveness Factor: Forgive yourself and others. Holding onto grudges and resentment is toxic. Let go of the past and move forward.

It wasn't about becoming a social butterfly. It was about nurturing meaningful relationships, deepening existing connections, and creating a support system that enriched her life.

Billie started small. She reached out to a friend she hadn't spoken to in months. They met for coffee, talked for hours, and rekindled their friendship.

She scheduled regular game nights with her friends. She looked forward to those evenings, the laughter, the camaraderie, the break from the pressures of work.

She practiced active listening. When she was with someone, she put her phone away, made eye contact, and truly listened to what they were saying. She found that her conversations became more meaningful and more fulfilling.

She allowed herself to be vulnerable. She shared her struggles with her friends, her fears, her insecurities. She was surprised by the support and understanding she received.

She expressed her appreciation. She told her friends why she valued their friendship, how grateful she was for their presence in her life.

She forgave herself for neglecting her relationships in the past. She let go of the guilt and resentment, and concentrated on building a better future.

Slowly, gradually, something amazing happened.

Her stress levels decreased. She felt more supported, more connected, and less alone.

Her happiness increased. She experienced more joy, more laughter, and more meaning in her life.

Her resilience grew. She knew that she had a support system to lean on during difficult times, people who cared about her and had her back.

She discovered that connection wasn't a distraction from her goals. It was a source of strength, a foundation for her well-being, and a pathway to a more fulfilling life.

Billie finally connected the dots.

You can't do it alone.

Nurturing meaningful relationships is essential for managing stress, enhancing your happiness, and living a more connected and fulfilling life.

And sometimes, the most powerful thing you can do is to simply... reach out.

Chapter 19: Small Steps, Big Wins

Billie looked back at her journey. It hadn't been a dramatic overnight transformation. There hadn't been a single, earth-shattering moment that had magically erased all her stress.

It had been a process. A series of small steps, taken consistently over time. A collection of tiny victories, accumulated day by day.

She thought about all the things she'd done.

- She'd learned to recognize her triggers.
- She'd mastered the 60-Second Stress Buster.

- She'd exposed the Time Bandit and reclaimed her time.
- She'd harnessed the power of "no."
- She'd rediscovered her "yes."
- She'd embraced micro-adventures.
- She'd started celebrating her "dones."
- She'd staked those energy vampires.
- She'd delegated, even when it was hard.
- She'd made sleep a priority.
- She'd fueled her fire with healthy food.
- She'd moved her body with joy.
- She'd trained her mind for resilience.
- She'd unplugged from the digital noise.
- She'd embraced the unexpected.
- She'd deepened her connections.

Each step had been small. Each change had seemed insignificant on its own. But together, they had created a profound shift in her life.

She thought about the concept of compounding. The idea that small, consistent actions, repeated over time, could lead to exponential results.

It was like investing money. A few dollars invested each day might not seem like much. But over years, with the power of compounding, it could grow into a significant sum.

The same principle applied to her stress-busting journey. Each small step she'd taken had compounded over time, creating a powerful momentum of positive change.

She wasn't perfect. She still had moments of stress. She still faced challenges. But she had the tools, the strategies, and the mindset to navigate them with more grace and resilience.

She realized that the key wasn't to strive for perfection, but to prioritize progress. To celebrate the small wins, to learn from the setbacks, and to keep moving forward, one step at a time.

She decided to formalize this approach. She created a "Small Steps, Big Wins" journal.

Each day, she wrote down three small steps she had taken to reduce stress and increase joy. They didn't have to be major accomplishments. They could be as simple as:

- Took three deep breaths.

- Said "no" to an unnecessary request.
- Spent 15 minutes reading for pleasure.
- Called a friend.
- Ate a healthy meal.
- Went for a walk.
- Practiced gratitude.
- Went to bed on time.

She also wrote down one "big win" for the day. This could be a larger accomplishment, a significant breakthrough, or a moment of particular joy or gratitude.

The journal became a powerful reminder of her progress. It helped her to stay motivated, to track her growth, and to appreciate the cumulative effect of her small steps.

She discovered that the "Small Steps, Big Wins" approach wasn't just about managing stress. It was about building a life. A life filled with purpose, joy, and connection.

It wasn't about reaching a destination. It was about enjoying the journey.

The truth hit Billie like a freight train.

You don't have to make dramatic changes overnight to transform your life.

Small, consistent steps, repeated over time, can lead to remarkable results.

And sometimes, the most powerful thing you can do is to focus on the small wins, celebrate your progress, and trust the process.

LESS STRESS: MORE YES

Chapter 20: a Stress-Free Sanctuary

Billie looked around her apartment. It was... different.

Not the cluttered, chaotic mess it once was. Not the sterile, temporary space it had been during the flood repairs. It was... a sanctuary.

Calm. Peaceful. A reflection of her inner transformation.

She'd intentionally designed it to be a stress-free zone, a place where she could relax, recharge, and reconnect with herself.

The colors were soothing. Soft blues, greens, and neutrals. The lighting was warm and gentle. Natural light during the day, soft lamps in the evening.

The furniture was comfortable and functional. A plush sofa, a cozy reading chair, a sturdy desk. Everything had its place.

Clutter was banished. Surfaces were clear. Everything she needed was easily accessible, but nothing was on display just for the sake of it.

She'd incorporated elements of nature. Plants, a small water feature, natural materials like wood and stone. She'd created a sense of tranquility and connection to the outdoors.

Her bedroom was a true sleep sanctuary. Blackout curtains, a white noise machine, a comfortable mattress, and a complete absence of screens.

Her bathroom was a spa-like retreat. A rainfall shower-head, aromatherapy diffusers, soft towels, and a collection of calming bath products.

Even her workspace was designed for priority and productivity. An ergonomic chair, a clutter-free desk, good lighting, and a separate area for creative projects.

She'd extended the principles of her stress-free sanctuary beyond her apartment.

Her car was organized and clean, with a calming playlist and essential items within easy reach.

Her office was personalized with plants, artwork, and a comfortable chair. She'd also negotiated with her boss to create a more flexible and less stressful work environment.

Her digital space was decluttered and organized. A clean desktop, a well-organized file system, and a streamlined inbox.

She'd created boundaries. She protected her time and energy, saying "no" to things that didn't serve her, and prioritizing activities that brought her joy and connection.

Her life had become a stress-free sanctuary. Not a place devoid of challenges, but a place where she felt safe, supported, and empowered to navigate those challenges with grace and resilience.

She realized that creating a stress-free sanctuary wasn't about escaping from the world. It was about creating a home within herself, a place of inner peace that she could carry with her wherever she went.

That was the moment Billie grew up a little.

Your environment plays a significant role in your stress levels and your overall well-being.

Creating a stress-free sanctuary, both in your physical space and in your life, is essential for managing stress, enhancing your happiness, and living a more peaceful and fulfilling life.

And sometimes, the most powerful thing you can do is to create a space where you feel safe, supported, and at home.

Chapter 21: Cultivating Calm

Dirt. That's where it started. Just plain old dirt, delivered in bags to her tenth-floor sanctuary. Billie surveyed her tiny balcony, a concrete rectangle jutting out into the grey cityscape.

She slipped on her gardening gloves, the old fabric feeling good and familiar on her hands. She looked around at her little collection of pots—her tiny green world. It was bursting with color, even though it was small. The bright red flowers of the geraniums tumbled over the sides of their pots, a real pop of life against all the city buildings. The little basil and rosemary plants looked like tiny green trees and smelled like summer was just around the corner. And yeah, even in her pots, those annoying weeds were sneaking in. Pulling weeds wasn't exactly fun or fancy, but there was something really satisfying about it. It was like you were actually in charge of making things neat and tidy in a private world that could slip out of control.

It all began with something she read online. It talked about how even small-scale gardening, like tending to pots on a balcony or windowsill, could have a big impact on your brain. Something about the way different senses – the smell of the earth, the feel of the leaves, the sight of the growing plants all worked together to calm your mind. It wasn't about becoming some expert botanist; it was just about connecting with something real and alive. A little green escape.

A ladybug with its bright red and black shell landed right on a basil leaf. Billie watched it slowly walk along. It made her think that even in the middle of the busy city, life finds a way to hang on.

For the next half hour, Billie just hung out with her plants. She gave them water, talking to them softly like you would a pet, as the dry soil soaked it up. She gently snapped off the dead flowers, like she was helping them feel better and grow new ones. "You'll be okay," she'd say to a droopy bit. When she touched the fuzzy leaves of one plant, it felt so soft it pulled her away from her thoughts.

A while later, Billie sank onto a small folding stool, her hands still slightly damp with the smell of soil clinging to her skin. Looking at her tiny balcony garden, bursting with life and color, she felt a sense of peace. This is where calm takes root.

She picked a basil leaf and inhaled its peppery smell. Then plucked a ripe, red cherry tomato and popped it in her mouth. It burst with sweetness. Just those little things. Sometimes that's all you need.

A quiet wisdom settled over Billie.

A tiny balcony, a few pots of soil, and the simple act of nurturing life are a powerful antidote to the stresses of modern life—and a direct route to cultivating calm.

Turns out our brains are screaming for green amidst the grey. So, find your green, even if it's just a single, fragile seedling unfolding on your windowsill. Plant something. Anything. Let the simple act of nurturing life remind your heart what peace feels like, one green shoot at a time, right there in your own little sanctuary.

LESS STRESS: MORE YES

Chapter 22:
Free Your Spirit

The late afternoon sun casts a warm, golden glow across Billie's balcony. A gentle sea breeze rustles the leaves of the potted geraniums, carrying the distant sound of children laughing on the beach.

Challenges still come. Life still throws punches. But now she ducks. The 60-Second Stress Buster? Her go-to. A few breaths, then clarity.

Her days are no longer a frantic scramble against the clock. The Time Bandit Busting Protocol is solid gold. Cut the waste. Grab the time. Do what matters.

And yes, the "Yes" Inventory has been a revelation. Saying "yes" had once felt like an obligation, now it is a conscious choice, aligned with her values and her well-being. The power of a gentle "no" to the things that don't resonate is unexpectedly liberating, creating space for more heartfelt "yeses."

Her journal is filled with satisfyingly ticked-off items on her Done List. Shifting from "to-do" to "done." Small wins. Real progress.

Energy Vampires have faded away. Not through confrontation, but through a gentle rebalancing of her time and energy. Less drain. More life.

And then there is Delegation. Hard. But she does it. Learning to trust others, to share the load, frees up her time, fostering collaboration and connection.

The most fundamental shift? The unwavering commitment to taking care of herself. The consistent sleep? Non-negotiable. Nourishing meals and joyful movement. Not luxuries, but the very foundation upon which everything else rests.

The gentle rhythm of her breath, a practice honed through Mindfulness and Meditation, has become a constant source of calm amidst occasional storms. Learning to observe her thoughts without judgment gives her a newfound sense of inner peace.

Even her relationship with technology has transformed, thanks to the mindful Digital Detoxes regularly embraced. Stepping away. Real moments. Real connections.

And through it all, the unwavering presence of close friends and family. A constant source of strength and joy. Connecting with others, sharing laughter and support. Belonging.

Billie stands tall, the lessons not just learned, but lived. The stress has receded, replaced by a vibrant sense of purpose and a deep wellspring of joy. Her future stretches before her, not as a daunting expanse of obligations, but as an open horizon of possibilities, navigated with a heart that is lighter, a voice that is clearer, and a spirit that is finally, gloriously, free.

LESS STRESS: MORE YES

The "Yes" Revolution

Billie stands before a group of people. Not colleagues. Not clients. But an audience of people who have come to hear her story. People who are struggling with stress. People who want to find their own "yes."

She isn't a guru. She isn't an expert. She is just... Billie. A woman who transformed her life, one "yes" at a time.

She shares her journey. The overwhelm. The anxiety. The constant feeling of being trapped. The gradual awakening. The small steps. The big wins.

She talks about the tools she uses. The 60-Second Stress Buster. The Time Bandit Busting Protocol. The "Yes" Inventory. The Done List Revolution.

She talks about the challenges she faced. The energy vampires. The unexpected curveballs. The moments of doubt and setbacks.

She talks about the lessons she learned. The importance of setting boundaries. The power of connection. The necessity of self-care. The art of embracing the unexpected.

But most of all, she talks about the "yes."

The power of saying "yes" to life. To joy. To adventure. To connection. To self-care. To the things that truly matter.

She encourages them to find their own "yes." To identify their triggers, to challenge their limiting beliefs, to step outside their comfort zones, and to create a life filled with meaning and purpose.

She doesn't offer a quick fix or a guaranteed solution. She offers a framework, a set of principles, and a collection of strategies that worked for her.

She empowers them to take control of their own lives, to make their own choices, and to write their own stories.

The response is overwhelming. People are moved. Inspired. They share their own stories, their own struggles, and their own hopes, and a sense of community is created. A shared understanding. A collective commitment to living a life with less stress and more "yes."

Billie realized that her journey wasn't just about her. It was about something bigger. It was about a movement. A "yes" revolution.

It wasn't about rejecting responsibility or ignoring challenges. It was about consciously choosing how to respond to those challenges. It was about living with intention, with courage, and with an open heart.

It was about saying "yes" to life, in all its messy, beautiful, unpredictable glory.

Billie continues to share her story. She writes. She speaks. She connects with people from all walks of life. She helps others find their own "yes."

She discovered that the more she gave, the more she received. The more she connected with others, the more connected she felt to herself. The more she said "yes" to life, the more life said "yes" to her.

And so, Billie's journey continues. Not as a lone wolf, but as a catalyst. A spark that ignites fire in others. A voice that inspires a revolution. A revolution of "yes."

Billie added another scar—and another insight—to her story.

Your story has the power to inspire others.

By sharing your journey, your struggles, and your triumphs, you can empower others to find their own voice, to embrace their own "yes," and to create their own extraordinary lives.

And sometimes, the most meaningful thing you can do is to start a revolution. A revolution of hope, of courage, and of unwavering belief in the power of "yes."

Also by Nicholas Boothman

Spontaneous Success is Everywhere

Earth Angels & Magic Moments

Convince Them in 90 Seconds or Less

How to Make People Like You in 90 Seconds or Less

How to Make Someone Fall in Love with You in 90 Minutes or Less

The Irresistible Power of Story Speak

Writing Madly - How to Write a Saleable Book in 10-Minute Bursts of Madness

About the Author

Nicholas Boothman is a true Renaissance man who defied convention by reinventing himself five times in 47 years, each time in 24 hours or less.

His journey has taken him from a high school dropout to a fashion photographer with studios on three continents, and then to a bestselling author with nearly 4 million books in print. But that's not all – he's also a motivational speaker who has inspired millions on every continent, and a champion for human potential in rural communities. Amidst all these pursuits, Boothman has nurtured a loving family with his wife of 53 years and raised five children, all while running a thriving working farm.

He has taught his revolutionary techniques of "Spontaneous Success" to thousands of corporations and colleges around the world including the Harvard and London Business schools. His first two books, How to Make People Like You in 90 Seconds or Less and Convince Them in 90 Seconds or Less have been translated into more than 30 languages.

LESS STRESS: MORE YES

Acknowledgements

This book owes its existence to the invaluable support and contributions of numerous remarkable individuals who, like unexpected gifts, spontaneously entered my life, ignited paths I never could have foreseen, and then, with some exceptions, faded away.

Among these amazing individuals are Jane Somerville, José Prazeres, Sharon Giannone, Dorothea Helms, Kerri King, Tim Whyte, Sandra Topper, and Lynda Hill.

Additionally, I am thankful to those who supported me with their steadfast patience and unwavering radiance, including Mike Freedman, Jason King, Dr. Claire Murphy, Vesa Villander, Sheldon Rudner, John and Lizzie Blackburn, Joanna, Kate, and Pippa Boothman, and Thomas and Sandy Pinto Basto.

And Wendy, of course, who always lights the way.

www.ingramcontent.com/pod-product-compliance
Lightning Source LLC
Chambersburg PA
CBHW070737020526
44118CB00035B/1468